TALL AS
YOU ARE TALL
BETWEEN THEM

ANNIE CHRISTAIN

Printed in the United States of America

First Edition

2 3 4 5 6 7 8 9

For special discounted bulk purchases please contact C&R Press sales@crpress.org

Cover Art "Fleeting Déjà Vu" by Eugenia Loli
Cover and interior design by Tiarra Gadsden

Library of Congress Cataloging-in-Publication Data

ISBN: 978-1-936196-61-6
LCCN: 2016930893

C&R Press
Conscious & Responsible
www.crpress.org

To Marcia:

Who will turn to this page and have to say *yes*?

CONTENTS

Section Three

Notes

Acknowledgments

TALL AS
YOU ARE TALL
BETWEEN THEM

They and the previously mentioned members of the Corps Saxonia treated the whole affair going on in my head merely as a continuation of the old feud between members of the Corps and the Students' Union. There were also Dr. Wächter, who was to take up a position of leadership on Sirius, Dr. Hoffmann, who was to take up a similar position on the Pleiades and who therefore, having been dead a long time, appeared already to have reached a higher degree of Blessedness. Both knew me personally in their lifetime and presumably for that reason took a certain interest in me.

Daniel Paul Schreber, *Memoirs of My Nervous Illness*, (57-58)

That two-eyed monster God is still above.
I saw him once when I was young and once
When I was seized with madness, or was I seized
And mad because I saw him once. He is the sun
And moon made real with eyes.

Jack Spicer, "Imaginary Elegies: IV," (32-36)

Section One

Two portions of her course had kindly well-nigh passed, and the seven stars [i.e. the Pleiades] had turned their shining car.

Seneca, Troades 43

The Sect Which Pulls the Sinews: I've Seen You Handle Cocoons

"[A man] shall not lie with another man as [he would] with a woman, it is a to'eva."

(Leviticus 18:22)

Silkworm dung lines my gums for tea;
I clutch menorah for paddle.

Malka, give me mother-strength
to save the scrolls.

I could never lie with Yôhanan
as I lie with women—

our chewing mouthparts,
our tongues just wringed fiber.

My holy sparks dwell in him.

The first time I touched a boy,
I glimpsed pomegranate arils
in the bowl
and felt beetles walk across my chest.

When I crushed them,
a monstrous insect leg broke
forth from my midsection,

ready to strike me at any time—
how I discovered my nature.

With faith, I could have spat into my hand,
clapped, and scored myself with a knife.

Instead, I, the most Chinese of the Chinese Jews,
love Silk Maker Yôhanan,
who sees me as a dybbuk.

It's true I carve questions onto the bones
of a rooster during Passover
and leave my doorpost bare.

You bring the smell of juniper and ammonia,
he hissed at my belly while breaking his tools.

I burned this foreign body once to please him,
but new and stranger shoots emerged.

I imagine placing his hand there.

There is no Malka,
Just a mother who carved *Shalom*
onto my infant chest
before drowning herself.

Carry me away, Yôhanan,
if I wind myself up in the floating Torah;

the sign on my hand is twisted bark,
fringe, spooned over pulp.

I've seen you handle cocoons.

Wondering If I'm a Descendant of the Nephilim While Lying on a Merry-Go-Round at Prentis Park

It has come to pass, my back
    on a merry-go-round;
                is there another name for it?

Or here is a Valentine's Day box.

Inside, a photo of nineteenth-century Toledoans
        staring at a 9'8" human skeleton;

      wind; atomic sand fused to olive glass,
        twelve thousand years old;

           a vestige; primordial hands
    on primordial single-celled forms

spinning long jaws of wisdom teeth;

      my reworking of *proleptic* into symbols
for you to paint onto your body
           when it feels misplaced the most.

        Funny how subatomic particles
can communicate with one another,
despite distance, instantaneously.

      I look for clues like the salt shaker trick

where one must figure out which number
           corresponds to each pattern,
      as if the placement of the two shakers
means anything.

This is 1, this is 2, this is 3, this is 4;
what about this?

When all that matters is what is said:

What about?=1, And then=2, What if I?=3, Now we=4.

And if we realize there was only one shaker
the whole time

or that what is said
is only what we want to hear
enough to create? I find myself saying:

Place the tongue and peppercorns until
boiling in water
to barely cover the taste of _____

before I see you. Do you already know?

I must tell someone:
Yellow stars of flakes surrounding the pupils
are clues one has blue-green eyes.

I was serious in the bathtub
after the dead woman was ceremoniously
covered with quarters.

Rh-negative blood does not seem to follow
human evolution;

I buried the pinecone seeds I loved the most—
but in a time capsule.

A nun saw cologne trail a man as blue fumes
and felt responsible;

humans evolved the most rapidly

during an ice age.

Now imagine a woman covering a fallen
                god with cloth while he is staring down,

waiting. *What if I* feel your extra vertebrae
if I know where to look

and then barely touch the corner of a leaf
                            onto your lips
    to show you what it is?

                Now we forget *what about* your hands
made them cold.

Mayfly Satellites

"They think our heads are in their hands, but violent use brings violent plans."
"Welcome Home (Sanitarium)" Metallica

This is the town where I imagined myself
    in your bed
        holding the *You Are Dead* sign

I stole from the Out of Body Experience hospital,

        where the electrical stimulation to my brain
gave me the sensation of being hugged.

        I did touch all the right combinations
    of prison cell bricks for eighteen years
because I posed for photos with my thumbs
        up near my armpits.

My body dweller said this would happen—
that I would be transported back to this world,
        to this reward.

        As transients with useless mouths copulate,
    mayflies turn into mayfly
        satellite imagery—neon green,

and it's true here too.

To explain what I was then—
all it took was a couple of hours
        of missing time
        for them to film all my news segments
    for the entire year.

Remember how at the abandoned cotton gin,
        before the kids were murdered
by other people,

                I told you I saw the burning gas field
set on fire by the Soviets forty years ago,

        your bedroom exactly as it was in 1974,

        and what came from the undamaged
parts of my eyes:

a spider crawling by pretending to be two ants
                        fighting—its fangs disguised
        as another full body?

                        That made you love me.

My life and body then were just
                        one of the lives and bodies
        I told the doctor he couldn't see.

        He said half of me burned in the crash,
and I forgot the other versions of myself
                        were supposed to be perfect
        to show him he was wrong.

Think of me.

        I'll be eating packs of Kool-Aid,
waiting in your bushes so we can lock eyes
        while I scream *Bitch*;

the mayfly satellites calibrating themselves
                        on the damaged parts of my eyes.

I'm already projecting myself
            into your doorway by asking:

    What's this thing that has left my body?

        But until then,
here's to hoping the nightgown fibers
                    I planted in the woods to frame you
are still here. I need them to perform Reiki

                        on the transients I mutilate
since the conditions of my release
                    require me to stay employed—

    no; I mean so I can be near something you touched.

I'm getting closer to receiving
                what a wrongly imprisoned god deserves.

God Wants You to Go to Jail

We are the children, and there was a god who wanted a target; he was man, and God loves you. God chose to send me to the hospital, and I can tell you this: He created us because the doctors have to know how to treat injuries in the combat zones of Iraq,

and He was scared of us, Jesus Christ.

I'm going to tell you, so listen to me; you go to State Street, East St. Louis, and in your head and mind, and you'll shake at night, and you go to the absolutely and say: *Please just let them shoot me in the foot and not the heart,*

and that was God who dropped semi-automatic weapons down your chimney.

There was a god who told you to riot. He made the last hour with a strand of your hair. Listen. He made the White and Black protestors yell at each other at the Central Park Five trial, all holding signs written in the same ink and handwriting, all wearing ear pieces connected to the same god.

If that's the word of God, He will amount to me. If God told me you were going to start a race war, God saluted, and I back to him and that happened, so listen to me.

I saw the god who told them to tell you to riot, and these kinds of Black and White protestors always appear to us from the same van. So listen. The Whites act and scream things that are sick and mean and racist, and the Blacks act and say that those things are, and I saw both their hand signals for "camera on." They keep His commands and come from Him on TV.

The news coverage was made to appeal to you, Black young men, because you are strong, like me, and crowned in heaven, and that isn't allowed to happen on Earth without God. Listen.

When you know there were 2,000 Black slaves on the Trail of Tears, you know that God wants you to commit a crime because he makes you go to school where you never heard that, but the crack dealer knows.

I want you to pray for right now; I want you to listen to me and the crack dealer who were anointed by God and the CIA. I want to tell you God is the savior waiting for you to pull the trigger into his heart, and your heart, and your mind, and savior, savior, you'll go to jail.

Jesus, thank you, and people, I'm going to tell you for the last time to knock a grandma in the head. Thank you that you're the lord and savior, in your mind, in the name of Jesus, and it will save your life. You're my friend. Forever in prison in your life.

The CD Mr. X Gave to Me That Proves Everything I'm Saying Was Confiscated by the Police upon My Arrest and Sent Directly to the Ethics Department

"Fortunately for him, he had written down the pertinent information from the CD on his T-shirt, which he happened to be wearing while he was giving his testimony and had not washed in two years. He asked the judge if it would be possible for him to step off the stand, remove his shirt, take off the T-shirt so he could refer to his notes, and the judge, who was as shocked as the rest of us, said yes."

Cold Case Files, The Shopping Cart Killer

The police said: *Get out of the car*
                    and bring this era to an end!

There was a god who wanted this.

They put forty-one bullets in the wrong man,
                    so I had to be blamed for the rapes,
            even though all I had on me
        was a stolen computer.

In the interrogation room, the cops dressed like doctors
            and tried to get me to consent
to a mouth swab,

                but I saw the seven foot tall
        brownish light (Mr. X) who guided me
                    to resist everything.

It's funny because when the cops
            performed the four corners consecration,

they used Indian corn instead of British corn (wheat),
                    so they received unexpected nature-beings.

                        The God from the North was my ally
and not the psychic scare-tactic stalker
        they always use at the precinct

to put the pressure on.

            It wouldn't have mattered either way.
I'm the kind of guy with a pops
                who wore a cloak of the beast

                        and who made me chew sticks of gum
        laced with Phenobarbital;

            ingesting it is the best way to know Satan.

I stayed strong and used the record player
with the broken spring
                and turned it by hand
                        to play Methodist hymns.

Naturally I became a rap producer,

                but I couldn't go along with my boss
who wanted me to inject alcohol and sugar
        into the spinal cords of little girls
around my building.

The record label wants me to freeze all the girls
        so they can be shipped from Earth first,
                            to test the waters,

        and because young girls will be more likely
to maintain the peace in the new settlement

until the rest of the chosen tribe arrives.

Any rapper who doesn't go along with this plan
        devised by Quincy Jones will be sent straight to jail.

        He is the fake father to thousands of children
in the projects, but I can make it on my own.

                    I'm a computer genius,

        I was temporarily hypnotized by the Geto Boys,

and for the past ten years I wrote on my arm
        I'm messed up with sex
but told myself *I'm sexually marvelous*

        to program myself to have better self-esteem.

I'm a warrior,
and if you don't decide to make this handsome
                face a free man,
                        I'll fuckin' kill myself.

The Game

"To allow lactation, cows are kept in a near-constant state of impregnation."
"With Farm Robotics, the Cows Decide When It's Milking Time,"
New York Times, Jessie McKinley, April 22, 2014

I think the person who done this crime, done it two-hundred feet away from the known crime scene. We're talkin' about being beguiled into the robot that scans their torsos, a symbolic adoption.

He gained the three's trust by tellin' 'em it was all a game. I understand that sonic technology lashed into 'em three times a day, and the mechanical cup disengaged with a quarter left to fill.

We're not talkin' 'bout a robot that just gives you an ID tag; we're talkin' 'bout the three being presumed dead over and over again while they was watchin' a flickerin' L.E.D. so they could go below sea level to hell—

like what was planned for Isaac if Abraham wouldn't've been a pussy.

The man who done this never planned to kill 'em the full way, but if you got sixty to seventy people goin' in and out of there a day, you're gonna have some who pick up a negative association. No doubt about it. Lack of tech support, high stress, more mastitis.

Believe it or not, the man who done this crime found the social network of Amen the Light and clicked "like." Amen's in the light lookin' at us at all times, givin' us grain, bein' partial to us, and kickin' us out when our data can't get no better. And when you click "like," you better believe you're gonna fight twelve men at once and win and people long since dead are gonna breathe life again through your trauma.

That's the real reason why preachers are out to get us. They say: "Can I have an Amen?" They want to take away our ability to fight, and I never give away my Amens.

Instead of prayin' their way, I fashioned my own shivs with the guards murderin' me with them in mind. That's why I know that the man who done this had so much power that the three was just goin' to the robot themselves without no one askin'. No routin' gates, no nothin'.

That's the kinda man y'all should be looking for.

Most of all, what y'all are gonna find is a man who took some objects of devotions from the individuals, and he'll be holdin' 'em waitin' to be sent to another planet because he killed the three before dawn and that was the deal, and he'll be pregnant-like with anticipation,

but nothin' can come out of him like before when it had been comin'.

Just by coincidence, not once since I come here have I not been pregnant in one way or another,
and there's no tellin' what that can do to a man.

We Do This to Simulate the Function of Digestion

"Indeed We created man from dried clay of black smooth mud. And We created the Jinn before that from the smokeless flame of fire."

Surah Al-Hijr 15:26-27

She was stolen
and became the whites of her eggs.

Often, she thinks of the first automaton duck—

how the defecation pellets
were hidden away beforehand.

Now she reaches her own back
and pulls out stacked rings of washers
lined with her own plasma
even before they were placed inside of her,

to weigh down her hooks for colder fish,
as she tells her lovers.

She remembers it all,

even when NASA tinted her red
so others would find her uninhabitable,

even when she was placed with the little ones
whose parts looked similar to hers.

They told her she once was a cuckolded
blacksmith and asked her what mobile string was,

that day, most like the emotion *love.*

She sits.
Her arms seem more shaved of cells.

Ladies know she eats corn;
                         they cover her with sheets.

Jokes about Nepalese Villages
Mostly Involve Goats

Today's sermon was about the master who threw explosives, forgetting the nature of dogs. This story must be referencing young Pakistanis who confirm Bin Laden is a CIA creation. By nature of dogs, I mean *due process*.

Which part of any of the White supremacist documentaries you've ever seen did you enjoy the most? For me it was when the guy found a woman to love, and she took him to the beach and said: *Look, all these people are having fun, and they don't have guns strapped to themselves.*

I wear a sleep vest. I'm a SWM, 41, who knows there's a store with a back door that leads to a beauty salon. The store sells patterns for ponchos, sweater dresses, and candles—Burda, Butterick, and Ocean Theme; I can take you there. One time I watched a young girl at the store knock two candles together. I question the actual contact point of the candles now, but I'll be more observant with you.

Do you feel the entropy?

More about me: The bowling champion featured at Midway Lanes who's holding his jacket on his back with one upturned finger knows that jokes about Nepalese villages mostly involve goats. The jokes are cheap and stupid in my opinion, but I'd whisper in your ear: *Nescient.*

That bowler is I.

Do you know that Lammastide, a time from late July to early August, is when witch weddings usually take place? This, among other things, makes royal and political weddings very curious. Also? Hillary Clinton decorated her Christmas tree with Black Magick symbols.

Let's get it over with and watch a movie about Mexican masked wrestlers fighting monsters. I'll take you to the theater and pay for the movie with dimes I store in my shoe. My grandpa did that for my grandma during the Depression, so you'll know I'm being romantic.

Watching Our Other Selves from Afar and Influencing Their Course of Action by Touching Each Other for the First Time Here

From *The First Days of Spring* (1929)

Salvador Dalí

There we are.

I dissolve my hands into a bucket for you
          until what's left
                              looks like pinchers.

You're not alarmed.

                    You know the thick liquid
          is still connected to me

and has feeling.

                    I didn't even consider I could absorb
the essence of the bucket.

The bucket's been the witness
                    to many murders.

It likes to be filled with skeptics
                    and dismantled wallpaper
          pasting machines. It wonders
                              how it can make its surface
                                        feel like toast.

I can survive as long as the bucket
isn't moved too far from my body.

I can't stop the bucket
          from being moved too far from my body.

          You squat to hold me up.

The way your shirt wraps around you
          without any buttons
     reminds me:

Are the crows taking away and returning
          your Aztec thought-form
               for my benefit?

Those boots must be projecting you.

Two crickets reproduce below the underage
flapper girl tattoo on a non-resisting
          man's partially shaved head.

This excites you.

          You bite the elastic band
holding my face,

     you draw me closer with your legs
               as if you don't have fingers
either. My drippings become tubers;

          the framed baby wants to understand.

Any second now a tuber
          could be stolen, and I'd die,

     but no one prepared me
               for what would happen
          when I stopped holding my knees,

thinking *Yes, yes* for you.

You're also the little girl holding
    out her paper bag offering.

Everyone says *no,* and your shadow
    reveals you're holding nothing,
        not even your arms.

I make the monk ask you:

    Why don't people tabulate every lack of
        profit so the mark becomes one?

        Everyone else's shadow is the suited man
straddling the other suited man
    who's lying on top of a skeleton,

watching and wanting
    and wanting your every move.

Done When No Longer Pink Inside

Of, supposing to,
       heat brackets on a bold
              face trench coat suddenly added,

informal as how turkeys run like us,
       as how the new law says turkeys
              are not to be killed or worried;

therefore, a vase cannot be thrown to break
since turkeys might become worried

              enough to remember they could be light
       enough to fly in front of others
to die without us,

              but first they must become wild,
like any of the various ways I dream

          of your morning hand
       in between Hume's long degradations,

the missing shade of blue
       really your hand
          in an infinite degradation of itself,

mostly in reds

as I wake to imagine I was right
          for no logical reason

            except for how I feel
when I make myself

feel near it, when I rub your mistakes,

when what is left has become *Architecture,*
analogous to finding the presence of your
neck in the trench coat collar
warmer than the brackets,

and what are they, archaic,
like the thoughts your hands keep,

like your wire hanger brought here
to be hot against all the others,

like touching the small of your back
because I read you should like it,

though lab mice are never asked what they
prefer and that could change everything,

asking you what you think of syllabic
dots until I'm not shocked anymore,

you, finally waking up to smile in a direction

beyond me, the quality of taking it to mean
mice always ask questions

when we think they aren't learning,

the swinging hanger derivative
of throwing out the results
when we agree we are in the best painful
variant form we never expected,

newly marked by how you ask me
why I'm wearing your trench coat,

my dreaming of flying through blue
　　　　vases to keep up with your changing hand,

　　　　to talk to your hand
as with my hand, see map of India,

practicing the principle
　　　　that every day is anywhere else,

　　　　hoping you're happy as I am warm
　　　　　　with your tempering, refinement,

　　　　　　　　the habit of imagining mice
turning into turkeys

　　　　　　into your hand I trace on paper
with the reddest plume without comparison

　　　　for you and I to reach for
　　　　　　　　with your hand
　　　when it leaves and returns,

realizing I must be acknowledging
　　　　　　even now I miss you,

done when no longer pink inside, etc.

Tie the Gamelan I'm Sending You Piece by Piece Up to the Heavens

Because of Fukishima,
I'm living out all the Brando outtakes
                    from *Apocalypse Now,*

         carrying Bacardi Breezers in my pockets
with three-hundred ghosts in each bottle.

The Indonesian tropical atmosphere
              keeps out most nuclear particles,
                        but men in the living room strobe in and out,

              pray, and reach out at me with umbrellas
                        that have plutonium on the tips.

My own leg tangled in a human
                    hammock washes in from the shore.

It must be Ramadan.

You'll die when I fucking say you'll die
                    I'm sure they say to me in Javanese.

Because my roommate says:
That's how you fucking peacock, I start to dress
                    like the Ramadan men.

              Though I had my first sexual
experience later than most guys,

                        I did see Russian women get caned
              in a basement when I was young,

so I'm not that far behind my contemporaries.

I dyed my hair blond just for this—
            to get the hottest Indonesian women
                              to tie me down and beat me.

                        When my brother was overdosing,
            I had a dream of him as a toddler
facedown on a parade float—

a single white sheet flying from the mast. Cocooned
statues were in all the trees,

            and it was my job to use rods
                        to keep all the parade items off the power lines.

He could have been anything—
            a man who threw out all the metal items
from his workplace window to pick up
                        and exchange for money after his shift,

            a rapper using razor blades
to create a talcum powder outline of all the continents,

                        someone who immediately thinks "militarized
            police" when garbage men drag bags of trash
against the pavement outside our house.

My life was too good for too long.

The next time you see me,
I will have been buried for a week,
                        slowing down my heart rate

            with at least fifteen photos of Saddam Hussein's
jowls in my pockets.

It's doable.

                        In the meantime, I am making you responsible
for turning on music I can leave to.

Sometime Under Prague

"I am sure that mushrooms in dropping their spores make a sound . . . . "

John Cage

In 1980, I knew that everyone has own plan, so I looked through video lens aimed at Tarzetta cupularis mushroom, and then I felt as if I was actually in very slow pace. I told cameraman: "Maybe you hear relief . . . . Can't you hear some relief?" He just told me I was speaking to someone who did base camp and who created whole concept for robot. I did not trust him with my thoughts—he probably suppressed uprising in Plzeň—so I picked the mushroom and left at noontime latest.

Later, I found out that cameraman was paid through Ministry of Culture. Of course, he's such, you know . . . black bird pecking eye of Turk. I put mushroom on table at my house, prayed, and I knew this was head of John Lennon placed in mushroom with help of special committee.

John said he had to be in mushroom because too many saints were created in fourteenth century. Five golden stars showed around his head—the number of so-called people who were him in life. Him being only one John was most frankly believed lie even during Communist Era.

This John played music something like Alice of Wonderland deflecting rabbit skulls inside bone church of Black Plague. He could play anything based in classical, jazz, sometimes even the sounds of honey comb goldfields from Scandinavia.

With the skill, I had to like him even if I didn't know him, but one time he made my house turn into so-called forest glass. He said it was to promote honor and peace in matter of fact. When he had big crown on his head and said in Latin "Let this house be blessed," he blessed it with what, you know?

So to make long story short, through other testimony of mushrooms since that time, the original Paul was pushed out of Charles Bridge, which created tourism as industry with help of ropes and containers. That is if I can believe monsters, you know holy knuckles, theos decorated with crabs.

I can say this so many times, but people went to where I discovered Tarzetta cupularis mushroom of John and picked handfuls of earth and ate it. They became flamboyant, full of life, full of spirit, some even burrowed in that spot, but those guys never lost their baby skull.

The legend is based on facts, but I don't do promises.

LAPD, Blue Child, and Low Daily Rates:
No One Was Killed in the Square

"A woman from Samaria came to draw water. Jesus said to her 'Give me a drink' for his disciples had gone away into the city to buy food."

(John 4:7)

There were three factions: the students, the workers,

 and the militants who were given bags of cash
 and Molotov cocktails
from the Invisible Light Agency.

 No one was killed in the Square,
but Blue Child's death spread all the way

   to the mother river of our people.

Understand this controlling need,
  the need to reproduce
 their own deviant hearts.

The Western reporter asks:
 What does a man blocking the path
   of a tank say to you?

Paid militants burned the innocent Chinese
  soldiers first and hung the corpse-heads
 from the overpasses, says a ghost?

The police lift the cistern lid to remove Blue
Child's naked body,

and the Invisible Light Agency next door
  block all electronic devices

within a ten mile radius.

They could have killed any one of us.

Way back during their homestay,
                    my parents recorded footage
of those madmen terrorists in the Cecil Hotel,

Richard Ramirez and the like,

            broadcasting *Voice of America*
                            to China from the 14th floor,

so I still have evidence to work with.

                I will always sing the red song,
            and I would never seek
            to fool the monitoring body
just to hang out on the roof of psycho killers.

It's very cool and charming
            but beyond the mainstream for a reason.

My nineties generation enter the foreign elevator
                    because they are interested in the game,
            in Sheldon Cooper,

but many from that nation
            want to make all of our people blue children.

That San Francisco O'Farrell, Hyde, Larkin, Ellis block
where nine-year-old Mei Leung
            was raped and killed by Ramirez
when she went down to her basement
                    to find a lost dollar—

what must be meant by "the killing in the square."

Under John Wayne's Hat

Stalin and John Wayne play mancala and eat fish with each other as much as time allows, but they prefer to call the game *Mangala*, the eternal being of the Mande speakers in Southern Mali, Africa. They can't personally remember if they were present at their own creation, but both unanimously agree the stretching, tearing, and eventual consumption of membranes must be involved because the auditory and sensory effects of such an entrance are the most satisfying, depending on the accuracy of the current simulations. John Wayne moves a rock and comments, "Perhaps after Adam named his roving and non-roving environment, he had the honor of helping to remove the membranes to see if his names were right . . . uh . . . pardner." "What is this thing you call Adam?" Stalin asks and eats a rock.

Stalin and John Wayne never express their curiosity of creation tales in obvious ways, but when John Wayne calls Stalin *The Duke* and Stalin calls John Wayne *Koba*, they know that the interchangeability of their names implies oneness and that the familiarity of using nicknames produces vulnerability and the inevitability of more nicknames. Such oneness and vulnerability near a frying pan of frying fish leads Stalin and John Wayne to lovingly admit—through direct rock tweaking—that they are not afraid to know exactly how they or the fish began.

Mangala is the word of choice for Stalin and John Wayne because this eternal being used an egg in the creation process and mancala rocks are the best eggs Stalin ever tasted. Mangala created life by placing seeds in an egg-womb until he had eight sets of twins who worked together to become innocent fish. They were harmonious brothers and sisters of glowing numbered scales, Mangala knew and was. The fish's innocent potential soon turned into jealous, ugly ambition, perhaps in an effort to gain distance and distinction Mangala could and could not ever understand.

Stalin and John Wayne are disappointed in the fish and agree to only think of creation in terms of the day Mangala created himself and his desire for others. Their game ends with Stalin's stomach and colon full of rocks and fish, John Wayne's stomach full of fish and colons, and their inevitable retreat to the couch, which they rip of all its plastic covering only to find they are right—it is Mangala just like their new nicknames that are easy enough to distinguish.

After several hours of contentment, they are hungry and sick of Mangala. The Cold War begins again like it always has, and when Americans see themselves under John Wayne's hat,

it's such a relief.

We Must Kill All Rats Before We Can Kill Your Rats

When I'm up late mixing concrete, the little children who live inside the walls scratch out phoenix designs. I talk to myself to drown out their chants of *white devil,*

and never once do I mention the Revolution—only how the leaders put an end to starvation.

I explained all my problems to the apartment manager, but he just said: *We must kill all rats before we can kill your rats.* It's true because the police only wiped out the local cat population after they had reached a tipping point.

To talk of starvation—my mom stopped feeding me when I was five because she was too busy sleeping with men to get free rations of chocolates and cigarettes. No wonder I ask the gods for more and more offspring—

no one pays attention to just one emaciated child.

Soon I was allowed to plug up all the rat holes in my apartment if I paid for the cement myself. Word of my strong character spread to all the parents on the block with *left-over women* daughters. Every mother I meet bows and gives me soft chicken bones and eggs preserved in ash and salt. I only take them because it means less food for her.

The guards told me with pride that they help all the sick mothers on my block. Just in case it's true, I place bananas at the feet of Shiva gutting a mermaid-whore so I can convince the gods to make more mothers suffer alone.

I spend my time renovating my apartment, teaching English, shooting roosters bound to blocks of ice, or volunteering to improve society. Just yesterday Onion's parents gave her gold earrings and pushed her into the closet where I was waiting to finally give them a grandson. I paid for those earrings myself.

Her male ancestors stood on a cloud and cheered me on with their demands for a male heir. I told her what I tell all the girls: *I want to investigate your faith.*

Many of these so-called cherished mothers here sleep stacked in silos that once stored rice. I shook their hands while the director of the senior center snapped some photos. The newspaper article said I was a doctor from a local medical university doing routine check-ups.

Western man monitors health of Bao Ming . . . .

Her kind won't be safe anywhere in this world.

Thorns to Rescue Their Bodies

Today she ate water in the hose after he came and he want to ate water but she is girl so stop going to hose but he want to ate water so go to hose. Now please God my mom and my dad is kiss and proud of him please.

Because they hear what is most fun they were dirty boy. It sounded like "sop." Suddenly one of the girls knew blood in the bowl. The way she looked as if she played "Salut d'Amour" for people. If true, she had clap from everyone. I want to swim in the bowl. I want to read a book about bowls.

In the white room I see her red apple growing in the bowl. It is a little bit green. He punches it. It changes to the evil. This is a strange apple. I said he hits it. It changes to his evil and the rainbow cider. A mouse in the corner wants her apple. The mouse is a rodent of food. People is rodent too. I won't ever give my apple. I chew cakes where I am, but I don't put flour in the cakes. If apples of people had thorns it would be to rescue their bodies. I put the flour all over my body to hide.

Today my mom get sick. My dad put a piece of meat into my mom's mouth. I was happy. Even then I remember my baby fish is dead. Dad gave it to adult fishes because dead fish can be food for adult fish. Dead fish are six. I don't know why they are die. I look at adult fish, and then I look at Mom's sick mouth and Dad always, always putting something.

Would Once They Aren't in the Coffer

Mom says she can't let another thing
                    be done to him

              when a preacher asks for Dad's
      still usable eyes.

I spit up staged tar too late.

      But with Marge, once a bridge
           plank told everything about us.

I would have whispered into her neck:
                  Say: In the urn.

      Mina says thousands look at her from fields.

When they enlarge their tendons
unnaturally, Mina worries they might notice
           she can see.

      She wants to touch them anyway.

Finally, the woman flaunting
      chewing tobacco pasties,

      and the other woman wearing
          thigh-high boots and nothing else

throw lemons onto the highway.

      We came all this way for them.
Get inside their suitcases.

Would once they aren't in the coffer.
The "they" who turn our toes
the wrong way.

Pull out the sword from the inside.

We read they hurt it all through you.
I in the walls. I in the walls.

Grandma, where are the bars of soap you fold
into your clothes? The blank cards
you send us on our birthdays to reuse?

There's head through the head,
heavy, whose head he walk all.

Do you all watch after each other, Grandma?

They lick their claws through us for weeks.
We rest on the fast.

Dad's leaner; he walks through
to where he was. *All the through to ask.*
All you need, ask me?

I dream of Mina and Marge.

Ask for our oranges, the norm. Pray for even
the used. One morn as he sees it, the garden
all. Some people say old, go Rosen down;

the priests' outside chant mixes with this.
All the time since, where do you go?

I Took to Walking Down the Middle of Highways to Avoid Getting Shot

"AND Satan stood up against Israel, and provoked David to number Israel."

(I Chronicles 21:1)

"AND again the anger of the LORD was kindled against Israel, and he moved David against them to say, Go, number Israel and Judah."

(II Samuel 24:1)

Mom carries water out from the well
        to the washing machine
     ever since her new boyfriend restricted
her usage of house water.

A neighbor yells: *Your man beat his last wife*
       and left her for dead at the train tracks,

but Mom says she already knows.

     See, he's providing for us, she says
as we eat steaks he pumped with air.

I recognize his dinner prayer
as words Jesus said once:

     I am the root and offspring of David,
        the bright and morning star,

Lucifer. There are all kinds of places to go
     like hiding in a storm sewer
        by the highway,

   but I walk into a room I should not have.

Is it her face

or a goat with its neck pulled back?

Thrusting his head into her mouth,
he tells her: *When your uterus rises to my throat,*
I call it hysteria.

The infighting meth mouths
and butterfly netting tube of it all.

He did tell me once that Mom's head
is venerated by the Incas. She should have covered
herself with the leaves and brush
the farmer didn't till.

I was there all day in the standing corn,

so none of this can be my fault.
I hate your fucking guts, she yells at me
in between getting punched.

I had spilled toothpaste on the carpet earlier
is the thing.

He snips and bags her bloody hair
so the kids at Bible camp
can make Ojo De Dios, he says,
slipping into an Eastern European accent.

If someone did an autopsy on me right then,
they'd find all the acorns,

my own transient and such imbued

how to cook down cocaine look.

No doubt he stores our money in serpent idols
from Solomon's temple
according to Yahweh's instructions.

Still, she does leg lifts to stay shapely for him,
no matter which guy she's with.

        I tell her to only meet her men
                       in a police station lobby.

                I, myself, took to walking
down the middle of highways
        to avoid getting shot.

Is she thinking of me when, left alone,
I clean her mattress,

            too young to know
what cleaning products can't be mixed?

She finds me—blood dripping from nose,
            hair moussed straight back,

      my brother's Brut deodorant
rubbed into the carpet
               so I will smell like it,

           a construction paper number
      taped to my shirt for a sports team.

She finds me—a girl who has become a boy
           so I can take her for everything she has,

a punishment I want her to endure
        because she'll let me.

I sit tight no matter what mistake
        she makes around me in the night.

Pretending to Go and Come from Heaven by Fire

The disk we live on is going up.

My heart opium-dreamed in triangulation
                    when I first saw you,

so I thought you might feel the same way—

            like we are holding the ocean in.

        Then despite all available technology
that presents a round Earth,

on Tuesday, your smile displayed our tryst
                    in the true level of flats.

How foolish you must think I am
                since you're spherical
        most other times,

                but I know what passed between us.

When your lips move and twist
                    like ballite churches,

        I wonder, could I ever share
a round Earth belief?

Well, I went to the San Bernardino Mountains
and carved: *NASA is Babel,*

claiming and pretending
        to go and come from heaven by fire.

I did that, and then I saw my message
                on photos NASA claims are from Mars.

So, no, I could never truly
                walk on the slant.

                        Are you on the side of world conquest
                and the sun and moon
not being the same size?

If you don't share my feelings,
                just keep things as if this letter never
happened in your spinning ball world.

                There's only a wall of ice
        keeping me from going over the edge.

Section Two

With such torrents do stormy Hyades o'erwhelm the earth of Pleiades dissolved in rain.

Statius, *Silvae* 1.6.21

The White House Tapes

"There are aspects of my experience in Louisville that I will never understand. Deep down I suspect that you may have more answers about this than I do. I can never shake my belief that I was being recruited, and later persecuted, by forces more powerful than I could have imagined . . . . As long as I am alive, these forces will never stop hounding me."

Iris Chang

I – Alfonso Sosa

My working conditions improved quick until I was soon manager and one day surrounded by pyramids. A different voice, a kind one, said to me: *You know your home is Pleiades.* I learned the language fast, but I've had better. Yes, the two customers. I had to learn how to speak to both, but it helps to know English so I can help at least someone. The band clamped around my neck after the second hour. How to say *weather*? It reminds me of Phoenix without my ventilator. I want the heat the more I work the long burials. I want it close to me. I'm always wet, so hot. Hot sweating or I just wet myself.

II – Slava Menshov

My mother tells me: *Your life is just like your childhood stories of perfect life. I feel like I read you.* I'm sorry. I'm not good with lying. I could not write this life. In this life, I took trip to oval quarry. I had just turned forty and wanted to show my wife I still had youth left. I wore suede shirt and pants—what I came to think of as my uniform—and there he was, tall and cold and staring. I dropped my pickax when his body rotated to match direction of his head. And I dreamt about, um, geometric proof; I do it. Please, I do it. But instead I talked to him. I was forced to. I changed my tone but nothing. Nothing. Then he stopped as if he heard directions at somewhere else. He fell to knees. He was, his thigh and upper body didn't move. A golden ratio away by car and my faithful wife nowhere. Sometimes I wake up and see dark air sitting on to me. Most times I'm nice because I heard that irritates them, no, confuses them, but sometimes I get angry and abuse it. I know this is a bad way to speak, but I'm doing it on purpose. But the time it walked backwards, its body away on some travel, I loved it as much as I love my wife.

III – Stephanie Wolf

I miss fingerprinting done with actual ink, even though I never experienced the process myself. At the police station, the cop told me where to stand and for how long. I knew his arms were the result of what happens when a scouring pad is left in a shower stall. I wasn't surprised at all when he used the foot pedal to get the full spread of my print on the computer screen. Out of habit, I almost turned the page when he nodded with his hands full. I felt like I was having piano lessons again because I couldn't resist when the cop removed my glasses and started to shave the hair surrounding my ears. The hair of the doll next to me vanished in strips too, and when wires protruded from her head, I knew the same thing was happening to me. He asked me who should receive the prints. I said: *Release them to me*, but I walked outside with smooth palms void of prints, and the first thing I could think to do was hide them in the snow. But I didn't because there wasn't any. I watched a string-on-a-dollar-trick one time and never forgot what happened at the end. There wasn't any snow.

IV- Percy Cavendish

My higher-ups go on and on about how tired I look—at the most inopportune times too just to weaken my resolve. My only real friend is the overweight bloke who hasn't left the office yet, so he doesn't know all the pain he's in for. *Who's your mate then?* Crispin asks me daily. The way he interrupted our boss, just to ask what the word *segment* means, broke my heart. He tries so hard. The night they injected me with the new cocktail, I screamed, *Yes, yes, bloody brilliant yes* because I'm trying to corrupt their data. In actuality, the crocodile bent my fingers back as he raped me, and I thought I saw a universe drift away by photocopier. I wouldn't let myself be a part of it, though. I told my boss I felt a distinct tingling in my fingers and nothing else. During Crispin's session, he held nothing back. He told us the secretaries nick all the light bulbs at night and hide them away straight up their twadges without cracking any. He said the silver beings dart around lighting up the place, and that's what the sun would look like if we could slow it down beyond the moment of stopping. When he stupidly eats his afters at lunch, smiling and slapping my back, I do something like break the top off the salt and eat bits of broken glass. The higher-ups never miss a chance to straighten my bloody tie and tussle my hair, but by god, I never give that lot anything they can use.

V – Adelle Whittier

The people from my city are the ones who come to your city and say: *Well, back in my city, we do this.* We just want to say the name of our city, but I can't say it now. Architects design our houses so every room has a clear view of the street. Our literature and commercials encourage us to watch the street so we can change what happens there. We can't be exactly sure what we change, though. I'm not perfect because I looked away one time and a truck crashed, spilling all kinds of meat. When I looked back, I knew many wolves were fighting over it all, but I only saw a man with no chin or eyebrows. He had sharp rods for hands. He asked me from there, all the way to my house, if I would like to be without hunger for six days. I said *yes* and ate his wheat. Before I could even wonder if I was changing him somehow, I saw hundreds and hundreds of his people coming from all angles, mostly angles that frightened me. Of course, their eyes watered, and the buildings all changed to look like Epcot Theme Park. A little while later, some of them wanted to take over and judge my life. The cops came and said to them all: *This doesn't concern any of you.* Then the street was silent and empty, and the only view I had was of my car, upside down, stuck on two sharp poles in front of my house. After that the dogs would just shake and hide. I could never give them the right biscuit again.

VI – Alexis Hophauf

Diana, shuffling and hunched, arrived covered in a shawl with a pill box hat on top. One night as I was flipping through the television channels, Diana pointed at the wrestlers bouncing off the ropes and said: *Those people look just like my people.* At times like these, she smelled like kerosene. Another day she told me she looks weaker than she should because she had to regenerate her own spine. I think she just replaced it with parts she needed less. We were the most intimate when I lay on the ground and she pushed over the bookshelf in my direction. She was able to lie down next to me before it hit us. I wanted to see more and more of what she was capable of, but I worried I was using her somehow. I had roommates before, but they mainly showed me things about myself I didn't like. With Diana, all I could think about was Cassiopeia.

VII – Tom Neugebauer

When I was a boy, nothing scared me more than the thought of horses drowning in quicksand. I would say to my grandpa: *Let's play a game.* He never said *no*, so I blindfolded him and stole his cigars. I smoked them later in the treetops. Up there I didn't have to be buckled down like I was on the school bus. Truth be told, there are actual horses, and then there are the destroyers who sometimes inhabit the horses. I killed the bad ones by blowing my smoke sharp and fast and tearfully. Later when I heard the story about the possessed pigs Jesus let jump off the cliff, I couldn't pull my robe belt as tight anymore. Why did I have to learn by committing Jesus' same mistakes? Now as an adult, I know there are people who say they love horses like I do, but those people are found dead hanging above dry lemon wedges—their prosthetic hooves lined with speed. I need more. It's true I get a little thrill when I read the mythologies or flip through the coloring books, but I'm torn apart even worse after I clean myself up. At night I stare down the nostrils of the evil ones and tell myself not to kill. It's a type of activism I humor myself with to keep going.

VIII – Serita Compton

On vacation at Montauk, any time I had to leave an attraction I would cry. The worst was when I refused to tie my helium dolphin balloon to my wrist, and it blew away. I just wanted to have the responsibility of an adult. The beach became a zoo when I started ramming my head into the knee of the man wearing a tuxedo. All he could say was *touché*. I took a picture of him with my Mickey Mouse Polaroid camera and gave him the photo without even looking at it. He and his wife waited for the picture to develop, and then she said: *It's none other than Satan.* Her husband started brushing off his left shoulder like there was something on it. A crowd formed of people using their Frisbees to block the sun and eat chicken. *I can't stop shooting heroin*, he screamed. In the distance a girl was getting her picture taken with a parrot on her arm, and she wasn't me. *With you, it's always something*, I told the man. I heard this from somewhere, and whenever I say it, people laugh, so I keep going with it. I ran towards the parrot, and my uncle took a picture of me with both of my feet in the air. We couldn't believe it. My arm sagged under the parrot when an old bum came to drag away a dead, bloated dog with red eyes, a beak, and pinchers. *I want to jump towards the atom blast if I'm going to be forced to fall back anyway*, he said. For the record, I almost drowned when I called the clouds *Snow White*, and I refused to change my shirt for the entire trip. My uncle told me not to tell my parents.

IX – Rossul Bakken

Once I was convinced everything would be okay if I could just look under every teapot in town. Last year Larry's got smashed, so he burned his whole house down. I stopped this from happening to me by using yarn to separate everything in my apartment—even pages in books. I had to show where one thing ended and the other began just like Mrs. Heinberger suggested. I see her every night. I wear a pea coat and weep into my head between my legs for it to stop. I love how she tries to outdo herself each time. Sometimes she ignores me completely when I'm there. I just walk in and stand facing the corner for a while until I'm ready to see. One time she was messing with a Ouija board. The cat's tail twisted like a crooked butter churn for sure. I know I was supposed to be scared, but everything everywhere else was worse. A red-robed figure only walked by in the mirror. He gave me a pock mark. Mrs. Heinberger told me she threw away the crystals that were supposed to protect us, and that was just like her. The funniest thing is that when we lay on her bed, staring up at the ceiling, we both panicked and fell over ourselves to get off. The ceiling was glowing, so I was brave and stood up on a chair to pick at it. It stuck to my hand for a while, and I screamed: *I got some on me! I got some on me!* But sure enough, they were just glow-in-the-dark stars her son put up the day before. Later we would touch nothing in particular and say *I got some on me!* for a big laugh. But that night when she rubbed my scabs, she said she could see violet fire on ram's horns. *Without bad, there can't be good,* she told me. A shadow snake twisted below us. How could any future marriage compare?

X – Gillian Casey

I have a story of Easter and Julio. A man carries a slaughtered pig on his shoulders past Julio who's tied to a tree in the middle of the road. Someone slings meat into Julio's mouth from a stick, and Mae wonders how so many teenagers can run past checking their glucose levels with their cell phones. Julio won't wear clothes anymore, so she hopes he never gets old. Mae feels warm and tired when they measure Julio's chest circumference. No one trusts him since he was found on a truck that possesses the technology to sense every human who rides illegally. He only did it to prove he is a part of humanity too. Julio and Mae used to be able to talk about the best way to kill moss on bricks like they were equals. Now he just tells her to watch out for Zizaubio and the Seven Sisters. He says if she calls them, she'll go into a trance and feel the white light who is Zizaubio. The Seven Sisters will be on thrones steeped in him. They'll say: *We're glad you came to Sars Ammith*. She'll say: *What is this? This doesn't match up with my ideas of Pleiades*. They'll disappear, and all she'll see is black for an answer. She knows Julio is right, but she still doesn't like being told what to do. My story of Easter and Julio means I always want Julio to be in the world in April.

XI – Alex McCorkle

The teachers were better than some I've had. I can't think of any complaints. They were better because each one managed to speak with only one voice at a time so I could keep up with what was happening. I never wanted to miss the display screen in front. When I was submerged in the liquids of varying temperatures, sometimes I'd see people I know on the display screen—like my mom staring into a mirror with her back to me. When she turned around, she had a mannequin face. She asked me: *What do you think?* She had just put on make-up. I told her I thought she looked like a scary mannequin because she thinks about herself too much. I felt like she was surprised I said that to her, but I could tell she was thinking about it to see if it was true. Outside of school I saw a movie preview, and when a logo flashed, my ocular bones became more prominent, and they're like that even to this day. When a triangle appeared under my left armpit, I told Mom it looked like the same one floating above me in Katmandu after I was submerged in the liquid. Much later at my regular school, my teacher asked us to think of three things we would do in order to escape a burning building. Three of us, including me, wrote: *Just die.* I think I remember being arranged around a tree with them one night.

XII- Dave Pinkston

Everyone always asks me: *Why are you so sexist?* I'm not sure I can answer that without telling this story. I sat in my chair and visualized myself walking around to see myself from behind, and it finally happened. Pop. But before that I found out many inhabitants of other planets watch a horror movie called: *We Know the Beasts Are Human*. Because I could see myself outside of myself in this way, I could see the blue skull-face lady too. She said her car is constructed out of pairs of dice. *This way, the car will descend down and down,* she said. And then I was in her fuzzy dice car going down, down. Her outfit changed to a fuzzy rearview mirror dice suit. *What were you before? You haven't always been this,* I said. That really got to her because she sent me back to a previous life when I was at the sauna with my father. The entourage was getting more water, and Dad had a heart attack. While messengers returned to the city to inform the officials of his death, I sent a psychic message to my sister to tell her the good news, and then Dad stirred. He had only passed out. *Do it,* she said as a concubine massaged her breast. I killed Father by holding his head as hard as I could with his nose and mouth and leg from behind. I caught all of his spasms. When I ran home, I put a cobra symbol between my sister's eyes and my own eyes so my copulation could ring fifty-two times. When the earthquake hit the palace, how could we not feel as if we were in a leather dice cup getting our comeuppance? After the vision, the blue skull-face lady twisted her foot into the ground like she had just had her final say, and then she disappeared. She did it stupidly—just like a woman.

XIII – Lynette Odom

I would say the quality of my love life changes with each new day. Sometimes I just have private dance lessons, but on my way home one night, I ran into a group of white-suited individuals. They were wearing wispy purple handkerchiefs around their necks, playing guitar, and pointing to a house up the hill. I didn't resist their pull because they looked like stewardesses, even the males. I saw their tray of iced coffee and took a cup, and just because of that, they felt like I couldn't say *no* to anything else. I was sick of walking around worrying about plate tectonics, so I agreed to go with them. When we got to the house, their skin got paler as they disrobed, and they rubbed ginger water all over each other's bodies. They held glasses of milk in front of wooden owl statues and clapped and got into tire swings when the milk appeared to be absorbed into the statues. *I didn't pour it out, but it's gone,* one man said. The walls were covered with collages made from photographs of our town and paintings of cataclysmic asteroids. My house was in the aerial photo, and I liked seeing it like that. My sweater had a dangling piece of yarn on the sleeve. I wanted to fuck everyone I saw.

XIV – Kipper Wang

Today morning, why the stirring is present when I'm on my bed? It was she's fault. She didn't do one thing that was arguing; I'll give her that, but I'm doing ridiculous thing now. I'm going to center of floor and leaning back. I put on any fire cap. I don't have time for this. I have to work the mistakes my brothers had made. I hoped to be famous when everyone found out I take cared of a deer. It was dead, but I couldn't live without. Blood came down from deer, but I prayed, and he looked at me with the same right eyes two days later. But she won't leave now, and my pelvic region rises first *So it will be more authentic,* she says. I floated three times and touched the ceiling, but things wasn't right. I ran to the bathroom and saw a baby on the toilet. When I returned, there was a bloody towel on the bed. I put out my arms. I attacked the beast as I punched the beast. The bed was now against a different wall. I couldn't open the door to leave. The most good thing was that I cared of the deer. I cared of the deer so much that I didn't eat breakfast anymore to deal with this things.

XV – Roy Harris

I was completely truthful on the job application and got the job anyway. The question was: *What's the best thing about heroin that people get too self-righteous about to consider?* I knew the answer immediately. I wrote: *Making the decision to need something more than anything for the sole purpose of actually having the means to get it.* The first thing my employers did when they came to my house was put my wife in the Freeze. She became invisible and couldn't move or speak, but I knew she was thinking about how we cracked open a double-yolk egg after her father's funeral. Right away my employers gave me LSD and asked me questions. *Where are you?* they asked. *I'm beyond time,* I screamed, *I'm beyond time.* They kept telling me there is no such thing, but they wanted to know more. They assembled the coils, and I ended up in the cabin of a Navy ship. They said my name is *John*, even though I knew it's not. When I came back to myself in my room, I was covered in green salt and fused into the floor. With my head still in the room, I watched two men place their hands on my wife. They instantly looked like they were drawn by children under the age of three, and my wife became reanimated. Ever since then, she can only speak in terms of Satan. Sometimes I try to pick up my coffee mug at breakfast and my hand goes right through it. My wife replies with something like: *Thank you, Satan.* We make a point to go to Montauk every year because the satellite images of the hyperspace cloud above the facilities remind me of home.

XVI – William Burton

Reading about the girl who died of exposure reminds me of when my wife got pregnant during the Depression. She had no choice but to go up that hill like all the other wives. She came back down, and I hated her more than anything for what she had to do. I hated her so much I killed any cat who tried to eat birds in the yard. I used my grandfather's Harper's Ferry Horse Pistol because I felt like enemies were riding the cats. I pictured my wife riding the cats. When my wife and I went down to Mexico, we fucked as much as possible in between my job as an exterminator. It came to the point where I hated to think anyone else but me could be fucking. We had ten kids down there, and five went missing. We all lay on the dirt floor and waited for the phone call. I had my cache of weapons, and I would shoot any cockroach that came near the babies—especially the ones I caught reproducing. I'd get the phone call, and then I'd wake up by the market with a bag full of human legs. Or I'd get a phone call and then wake up below young men who were chained to walls and always screaming *Dios*. Even after just waking up, that's exactly what I felt like. Now I cut everything up and put it back together like I did in Mexico. I cut up my wife's birth certificate and an essay on the perversity of Disney World, put the pieces in a box, and pulled out *Never been born*. My grandson laughed like I did, but he didn't know why. I laughed because ever since my wife did what she did, that's how I try to make her feel.

XVII – Celeste Heinberger

The first time I saw Rossul, he was walking down the staircase at the public library, and I happened to look up. I felt like he had just emerged from a meat locker. I wanted to add a fur hood to his pea coat and watch him cross the street from my car. He introduced himself by saying he loves the dark circles under his eyes even though his mom wants him to wear foundation to cover them. When he comes over, I pretend he isn't there, but I read poetry by Pindar to raise up the deities for the athletic festival we will make. He likes to hear stories about my life too. Early on in our contact, I told him I was visited by Iris, the angelic rainbow messenger goddess, in a dream around the time of my first period. Many years after the vision, when I was ready to undergo the initiation, my mother and aunt prepared a bath for me with special oils and then wrapped me in a black robe covered with pentagrams, moons, stars, and suns. At that point in the story, I could see that Rossul became aroused, and he made no effort to hide it. Continuing on, I told him I held the goddess crystal in my hands and met a guide who led me to a room. I waited there, and a figure I didn't know, but whom I later realized was Rossul, languidly walked down a staircase as if he were using his body for the first time and handed me a scroll that said: *How could any future marriage compare?* Rossul and I quickly became lovers after I informed him of our karmic destiny together. One evening he told me he did some research on Iris and found out she is a sister of the Harpies. He asked me: *Doesn't that make her a monster too?* I slapped him, but then I put a laurel wreath on his head to try and take it back. I love him so much that when I bring out the life-size human dolls, and we stab them every which way we can, I can't believe we really belong to each other.

XVIII – Cindy Neugebauer

Every boyfriend I brought home made fun of how Tom liked to play with horse figurines. He latched on to the toys even more because he hated those men. When he'd go to his dad's house, his step-mom got sick of hearing about horse stables, and a horse's lifespan, and horse grooming. Tom claims she locked him in a room and made him listen to the baby monitor receiver that was paired with the transmitter in her mother's bedroom. All the grandmother did all day long was say: *I'm doing the Masonic pose. I'm standing with my body erect, and my feet form the angle of an oblong square, so kill me now.* She was paralyzed, so Tom told me he stood in the way she described for as long as he could to speed up the process of her death. When Tom hit puberty, I was concerned he still kept his horse figurines around. He wrapped each one in a silk cloth and kept them in an old backgammon case he carried everywhere like a briefcase. One day when I was gathering up his bed sheets for the laundry, I found one covered in lubricant. I didn't know how to handle any of this, so I bought him a subscription to *Playboy*. When he got older, he incessantly talked about an infinite line of horses running through an infinite desert and all the froth they would excrete from their mouths when they were on the verge of dying from thirst. He imagined it as an irrigation system that could create lush vegetation he would like to live in forever. I've decided to let this all out in the open now because I finally told Reverend Colby I would sometimes see blue centaurs out of the corner of my eye when I lived with Tom. Reverend Colby said it's wrapped up in an evil, and he wants to help.

XIX – Woorim Kim

When I worked at the pyramids, I never became a manager, which is good because I wanted some time to think on my own. It was hard since we were in direct alignment with the leaders who sent me messages through the pyramids. In their feigned conversations with other workers, I also heard veiled messages that were meant to unnerve me and denounce my manhood. The leaders mentioned how they were to blame for all five of my children being born without their second and third fingers. The other workers got caught up in this campaign against me and spoke an enchantment until their eyes turned completely black. Then they dangled me by ropes above the cherubim power generator. I pretended to hate it, but I hoped they would drop me, and sometimes this hope would be the best part of my day. One time I got too close and had visions of soldiers being slaughtered in war. They wore chaos insignia so my leaders could spontaneously ejaculate at the exact moment of each soldier's death. When we capped the pyramids with gold, I would often wretch, and the bile would land in what I knew was the same formation of volcanoes on Mars, the three middle stars of Orion, and the pyramids we were building. Sometimes when we floated the stones, I wanted to crush everything and everyone in view so we could start the world again the right way, but my leaders were always there, their voices reverberating as if to say: *That already happened many times, and we were always there to start again.* No matter what they said, I could tell they were frustrated they couldn't get me to turn my eyes black like so many of the others. I touch my eyeballs every now and then just to make sure I'm still me.

XX – Crispin Stone

Percy's simply first rate. We've been chums longer than I can possibly remember, and he's only acted in my best interests, even when he wraps my bandages in a way that will never stay bound. I think all his low spells and grumpy faces are down to the lack of a ladyfriend in his life. Poor Percy isn't fortunate enough to have a woman to love, not like yours truly. Hana accompanies me on trips in the transport vehicles and rubs my belly and laughs when my head won't stop thrashing around. Perhaps I rabbit on about Hana a bit too much, though. Percy and I were having such a splendid time of sorting white gold dust into lines with razor blades, and then, at the slightest mention of Hana, Percy's mood went all to pot. I know Percy is often with her during break times, so I find it rather odd he doesn't like her more, what with all the time they spend together. One time I was walking past the office canteen when I happened upon the two of them, she giving him a demonstration on cadavers like he was some sort of prized medical student. How lucky he must have felt! She slit their throats and then cut and pulled out the tongues through the holes she had made. She placed the tongues in some of her mouths, started chewing, and told him this is what they did to traitors. I can't pretend to understand all of what happened, but I knew I wanted her fake eyelashes to brush against my face and for her to incubate her eggs inside me for once. She even notices when my injection sites need ointment, bless her, and I haven't told anyone this before, so whisper it, but I pick at the wounds so they'll get infected and she'll have to do something about it. Thank heavens for Hana and thank heavens for Percy when I'm back at the daily grind of being injected and telling my bosses about the fluorescent snakes being sold at the market. It may sound rather mad, but it always feels like I get struck by lightning if I don't at least bring something to barter.

XXI- Penelope Menshov

Slava caught my eye because I thought he looked like the first human in space, Yuri Gagarin. When I watched him eat his fish soup from afar, I couldn't help but think of the fish coming back to life in his stomach. I imagined the fish joining with bits of carrots and potatoes and whirring as if it had a motor. Our first night together, I put my head on his stomach and dreamed I was in Jonah's belly eating potatoes and carrots that grew on the stomach lining. I think this is why I fell in love with Slava—because he seemed like the only person who could keep a fish like that in his stomach and be an even happier person because of it. He was always doing things like beating his chest and opening the freezer to breathe in as much cold air as he could to make himself laugh. But he had passion too. I would find him lying on the living room floor at 3:33 AM studying sacred geometry, freemasonry, ancient mythology, and the Bible and clawing at his stomach while wearing a women's wig. The story I always tell people is that when I visited his mother for the first time, I stole the dress she used to make him wear as an infant and tacked it on the wall by our bed. I just wanted to feel closer to him. The night before he went missing, he sweated against me all night while moving his head as far as he could in every direction. He spoke in his sleep about Dogon, and Sirius, and the fish people returning to Earth in spaceships and how he could only fool them with his disguise for so long. When I asked him about it the next day, all he said was *I don't want to learn how to do metal work*. Sometimes I hear a voice call out to me saying: *Put on your dog star head*. This makes me laugh, and I don't know why, but it makes me miss Slava even more. If I had the strength, I'd sever my hand to show it how serious I am, but instead I often find myself leaning on the open freezer like a cane—my mouth wide open. At those moments, nothing is funnier.

XXII – Owen Pinkston

We just got a new HDTV, and while I like it, I keep a modified dust cover over it for the most part. My oldest son can't even stand it when his friends with HDTVs don't watch the right HDTV channel. He hates how the image gets distorted and stretched out without it. So when we watch TV through a couple of holes I cut into the fabric, my son gets huffy and slams things down passive-aggressively, but all I have to do is stare at him without blinking for a couple of minutes and he goes away. I just feel like I'm watched enough at work. I don't want to openly invite it with heat-sensing imaging surveillance. I try to do a better job with my youngest son, but one time he nearly pulled off the ID tag that's attached to my chest near my heart. My bosses change it every month because on the thirty-two day mark, lethal toxins would be released into my body if it's not replaced. Of course, ripping it off would produce the same effects. So when my youngest son nearly killed me, I slapped him out of reflex. I cried in my bedroom and drank whisky all afternoon because I felt so bad about it. My kids think I'm a monster, but I do everything for a reason they can never know. Once a night I wake up and can't remember at all how I wound up with my kids. I never married—I know that. Then I remember, but the memory seems glossy like a magazine ad, which makes me happy to leave and go to work the next day. I had to take a psychological profile one time, and I wrote that I feel like Pavlov's dog but without the luxury of hearing bells or eating. No one ever told me what this means, but sometimes I think they did. I can't say anything about it either way.

XXIII – Margaret Hophauf

I have a feeling I liked being around Diana even more than my daughter, Alexis, did. I thought Diana's hands looked beautiful like the hands of a male homosexual piano player. I made it my job to send her new scarves, back-braces, mirrored sunglasses, and varicose vein socks even when she had a full supply. I loved the slow and deliberate way she stirred her food and revolved healing orbs around my head. Sometimes the orbs would drop and she'd say: *They were working the whole time because of you, and then you thought about binding and gagging your enemies and controlling their intake of food.* I tried to improve myself, but when we were alone, I begged her to walk through a wall for me like I caught her doing once. She just looked at me intensely like the caricature artist in New York City who studied me for a portrait he didn't know how to draw. The next morning, I woke up beside a painting of myself pregnant with Alexis. My body was see-through, and both of Alexis' tiny hands were poking out of my belly and grasping at empty space. I took this to mean Diana knew I went to Tepoztlán and drank all the holy drink I could when I was pregnant. It was alcoholic, but since it was created by a god, my doctor said this was okay. Because Diana turned out to be a bitch, I spend more time thinking about Alexis and all the things she is capable of. As of yet, I haven't become frustrated at all by my daughter's failures.

XXIV – Jesse Gathman

I first started going to the meetings because I agreed heaven must be a pyramid inside the moon. I liked the sense of community too. We call our house *Megiddo House* because Megiddo is a hill in Israel where many battles were fought, and *Armageddon* means *Hill of Megiddo*. One day I had just taken a shower, so I knew I was outside. We had a great celebration there. One woman had heart palpitations, and with each palpitation, the campfire flickered green, and we all danced and clapped. During the course of my growth, many inanimate objects did things most people wouldn't believe. I loved it the most when the coat rack sat across from me, crossed its legs, leaned towards me, and just listened for a change. I love my family, never being alone, and singing in the public fountain with a plugged-in boom box. People shout and tell me not to drop it, but I tell them: *No, I have something to tell you. Don't you want to have sex at the Megiddo House to accelerate Armageddon and also have sex at the moment Armageddon happens? It just makes good sense.*

XXV – Grace McCorkle

When Alex was a small child, all he had to play with was an inflatable kiddie pool he kept stocked full of tadpoles from the creek. I was so dissatisfied with my life and surroundings back then that I took too many sleeping pills every night, and a few times I even used the thumbscrew I inherited from my mother—just to transfer the pain to an area I could identify and control. When it turned out that Alex tested off the charts on IQ tests, I thought that could be the solution to all of our problems. I finally came across a private academy, I know this sounds unbelievable, whose administration would pay us for his summer enrollment and buy us a new fully-furnished house just for his participation. It's true Alex's behavior changed after attending the academy, but I think it's just because he was learning discipline and becoming more like an adult. He reminded me so much of his father when he said: *My white blood cells are going pop* and then used his finger to make a popping sound with the inside of his cheek. I slapped him, of course, because I hate his father, but besides that I rarely laid a hand on him. The only truly bizarre thing I can't account for is that one night I found him sleep-walking around the house, and I swear I saw three pairs of legs attached to his mid-section all walking in unison. I just went back to sleep because I had had a stressful day and couldn't deal with it. The next day Alex was completely fine. Whenever Alex is away at academy, he mails me the most darling sketches of hell realms. They are mostly advertisements for space hotels orbiting hundreds of miles above the earth. On one he wrote: *Where You Might End Up,* and there's a hell realm. I think it's cosmic and folksy, in a way.

XXVI – Jan Engstrom

I try to keep an eye on the house down the street, but I can't watch too closely because there's always a face looking out from the top story window beneath a heliographic star. I think that's Adelle up there, but I can't be sure it's always her. I never catch her eating, but sometimes I see her brushing her hair. She never takes her eyes away from what's going on outside her house, which is usually nothing, except for one time. I was driving down the street, and when I got directly in front of Adelle's house, a tree bent down, playfully almost, and asked me if I wanted to be without hunger for six days. I was actually in the middle of a fast with some women from church, so I was very tempted. I know I should have been scared of the tree's sharp rods for hands, but his offer seemed simple, pure, and not backed by any malice. I said *yes*, got out of the car, and ate his wheat. I looked down the road, and the trees all started bowing to me, one after the other, dancing almost. One went so far as to suggest I build my own astral temple. Once it was constructed they all promised they would visit me. I was flattered by the attention, of course, but I was thinking about my husband the entire time. When I happened to look up at Adelle's window, she was dancing like the trees, and her eyes had no irises or pupils. I noticed many anomalies all around her. The strangest thing is I haven't eaten another bite of food since I ate the wheat. I just haven't needed it. Sometimes I worry that the trees modified time so six days are lasting an eternity, but I try not to let it keep me from helping others and shining the good light. That's all I can do really.

XXVII– Kipper Wang

Now things have gone too far. Once I was young, I didn't know words for me, but now I can speak and I will. It doesn't seem to matter I cared of a deer at all. I was at work and I started seeing colors' travel crazy. I felt sick. A ball of skin moved up my back. I thought my chair was unfit for me, but it fitted. I think the harm thing is coming, so I shiver, but I get tremble! I thought the ghost would be sleeping too because it's daytime, but I was wrong. How could I do bookkeeping? My boss looked like he was a turtle poised for a better phone, and I couldn't follow his words. Nothing was right. I begged my boss a break. Now I have no job. I don't like water in my watch. I don't like ripped cushions. I don't like flying dreamings, but look at my house. Sure, I have a deer, but my carpet takes me a prisoner. Deer, I love you, but now I just get in the way of my home.

XXVIII – Zhu Tiantian

After the radically capsizing situation I was mixed up with concerning great brother Julio, I tried to become a beatific rainbow person of the challenge. Being the principal of a school, I knew I had a solemn yarn capacity to reach a wide group of people for their enlisting and betterment. I knew this. I knew what an illuminated hair between my eyebrows could do for my life situation and the eyebrows of others. Yesterday I brought in all the teachers so they could chant around my desk. It was not a chant of hateful indulging cheek pits. I told them to look at my hand reaching for the bejeweling fortification for all generations. It's starting. I told them to honor my expanding eye of the wind deity crust. Do it as you see. I told them my voice is a chalice of teacups reassembled for the weaponization of space and protection. Yes, yes. I told them to adhere to my lungful feast all at once. I did. I told them to eat of my food so they would be forever dependent on microchip-tracking their children and dogs I tolerated enough for them to keep. It's stronger now. I told them to sit up straight in my lotus blood of intermarriage for soul possession by the snakes. Take over forever. I told them to look at their metal embryonic sacks and see if they could do better. Kill, kill. I told them Rising Sun, do what thou wilt forever and break the fools at your altars. Grow, grow. So when the community gets riled up to their boiling pan about the separation of church and state and bring up Julio, which I've paid for by genuinely crying about it in front of everyone's faces, I'm bewildered. I'm working harder than anyone for a New World, Hope, and Change that I won't explain or fully define until it's too late. But I promise, when it happens, and it will, everyone will be equally responsible. But for now, stand in the Work of the Ages. Cover its leaf with your genitals and eyes that still don't see.

Section Three

So does starlight splendour wane . . . and the huddled flock of the Pleiades vanish away when Phoebe [i.e. Selene the moon], shining with borrowed light, with encircling horns encloses her full-orbed disk.

Seneca, *Medea* 95 ff

All Your Best Key Chains

So the home business ended up costing you
                    forty dollars, twenty for the permit
            and twenty to the chain letter

        scam agency who gave you the materials,
                    and you made no money at all,

            and it didn't help you were in love
with a girl in your Buddhism class,

        and you're a girl too, don't forget,

and the more you thought about it,
                the more you realized that in 1992
when you watched the episode of Picket Fences

            where Kimberly's best friend spent the night
                        and suggested they kiss,

but when they did,
                the censors blacked out the screen,

and you wondered: *What girl would I kiss if
                I had to and would the world black out?*—

yes, that did mean something after all,
            but what kind of love was this?

You thought maybe this girl you loved
would think of you as the Ghost Festival
                        key chain she bought in Japan

    with the ghoulish face

she picked out from all the others

because she thought it looked kind.

And when you used a hook
        to remove your brain

                to hide the amoxicillin
in the safest place from this girl you loved

        because you told yourself you'd still love her

even without the possibility
                for thoughts of affection and sex,

you really only did it
        because she had a Pharaoh Akhenaton
                keychain and you could be the best

        This Is Your Brain on Drugs commercial ever.

You met with Akhenaton the day before
and gave him all your best key chains
                so he might chisel you

how he wants others to see him: warm
        with his family and possessing no genitalia

except earlobe *superior* genitalia.

                But your brain is in a jar,
        and Akhenaton is dead
like all your favorite obsessions,

so who was the round, breast-hipped
                man who jangled all your best key chains

in your face and the sun
until you fell asleep in his lap?

He whispered, *How great does it feel to hear you*
                    are like a snake
         in the hieroglyphics of "jump"?

         so you might dream about this girl you love
                    and ask her if she knows you're okay

because a snake also feels useful
              spelling what it can never do.

Villagers Chop Them in Half, Thinking They Are Snakes

"Come not between the Dragon and his wrath . . . ."

King Lear, Act I, Sc 2

"He thought the Beatles were witches flying on broomsticks from hell."

Dr. Phillip Joseph

In a network of underground tunnels,
     I created white mono-atomic gold
     because I refused to sit around on welfare.

The more electrodes I wore,
        the more I saw The Squire
     as the fabric cube my body formed around.

     My own fingerprints on my body
added to his mass. When the floor supervisor
     heard my heart monitor ring,

I told him I had to be the first person
        to spread out The Squire's fingers

if I ever were commanded
     to burn them with grease.

I was ordered to put black beans in every hole
     of a skull
        and water it with rum.

Beans sprouted. After the Holy Spirit Apollo
     yelled at him, I got my anointed pancakes.

     To tell the truth, Moscow's Coat of Arms
        appeared on my cheek.

I assumed The Squire's power came from Queen Elizabeth's
    stag beetle broaches.

                Soon I knew he was a Pre-Adamic man
who kept racism in Oldham

        and who prevented me
                from having a girlfriend for nine years.

I even wanted to crush him with the crystal
New Jerusalem that floats above the old one

                        thanks to the tall blonde aliens
                who masquerade as Jesus.

But Lord help me, as soon as my knife
                entered his chest, I saw him

—a Vedic yogi undulating knee-deep
in the monsoon-soils of India
                with legless amphibians encircling.

I thought, "No one deserves to die in shock
        from the knife of a farmer
                        who thinks you're a snake,"

        even though I stabbed him
    nine more times.

Queen Elizabeth, *Just let me be normal.*

Inside a Hand Basket in the
Burlesque Theater

As you may already be aware,
  the Burlesque Theater is upon us,

and the granite-encased monoliths
  of your muscular legs
    drilled to the sides of the stage

are as tall
  as you are tall between them.

They are your legs after all,
    and Victorian women know it,

  and advanced syphilis knows it,

and the shining temples
    of the man rubbing pistachios
  on his suspenders

know it's impossible
to avoid the thought of steam beer
  and a cast-iron stove to read by
    whenever they are easily distracted.

You have never been more happier
  to be more astonished
    that those are your legs,

  and those are people too
  who know your legs

more than two people

of Moorish personages
peopled through twin Moroccan peepholes.

                Those are your legs,

and all it took was a little foresight to realize
      you couldn't stay in an Extravaganza

forever where performers only act as if they're acting,
          they only think to use French obstetrical

atlases for all kinds of padding,
      and they only use their hands and eyes
            to convey the limits of one's scope

at arm's length.

But you, in your hand basket,
        use your hands and eyes
        as if you are signaling
            in the great conversion

from stage lights to sun
       to lizard skin

        able to keep what it needs from its past
to independently use all of itself

      until the crowd feels this potential
        of crests and spines as their own,

even in the dark.

You, who are flanked by your old legs
        that all agree
        are the only lines you'll ever need,

scream about marble statues
and how they should never come to life
because they'll never enjoy it

unless they can have it both ways,

and your song is witchery
embroidered in aurora
bands of sequestered dusk
for this night only and tomorrow too.

But the big difference is there is a purpose,
three-fold, peculiar, salient,

the mesmeric pull of leg and leg
and basket commanding all,

seducing all, until all comes
together in grand separateness,

and no pantomime had to translate how it felt
the first time you didn't feel alone

outside yourself,
perfect and imperfect;

the crowd clapping singly
with the drollest hearts and limbs of leg.

A Spider-Man Must Be Born of This Earth

With $500,000,000 in tax free winnings in my pocket,
    I clap at all the terrified children
        in hospital beds at the 2012 Olympics.

Bell Labs said that's okay.

        Your assassin training is all well and good,
    but I own the concept of the Yellow Pages,

and I changed my name to Samir
    after watching *The Ring*.

Have we ever stood next to each other
    without a geneticist present?

When River Phoenix couldn't stop pinching
    himself on his right side
at the army photo-shoot,

    I was having an appendectomy a hundred miles away,
        so of course he and I came from the same
            DNA fragmentation pool.

This DNA makes it possible for me to read
        all the unorthodox binary code
    that comes straight from God
through dirty electricity.

Insurance companies give away
    the circuit packs I grow
        so citizens can match the correct parts
    of their brains to the corresponding
seventy-two demons of Solomon.

When it works, it tickles AT&T to death.

I unfold your note:
Bill Gates knows that reality splits
every time a baby is circumcised.

I write back: *How can we ever truly connect*
during our breeding sessions
if the Navy keeps opening a time hole
in front of your genitals

just to destroy my essence of spirit
with an anti-matter bomb?

No matter what happens to me,
my teeth always grow back electronically.

Know that.

Never mind. The note I wrote to myself
and hid in my steroid pouch says:

They are capturing my essence of spirit,
digitizing it, altering it,
and then putting it back into my body.

When they captured it last,
I sat on a Gregorian calendar
soaked with menstrual blood
and went down to my core level
to take the elevator.

Two hundred miles up,
I looked through a telescope
and saw Nazis meeting together
to come up with an idea for our company flag.

It all started with the all-seeing eye of Horus
        above beams of light
they altered into stripes
                        and a star circle formation
        for you and me to have tantric sex on.

But I showed up here because Canadian citizens
                have to correctly solve math problems
        before they can claim
                Taco Bell prize winnings.

        I'm still alive because a Spider-Man
must be born of this Earth.

Orbs Whose Collective Sum Signifies My Age

Think of everything that has led to my seeing
        tadpoles eat strings of eggs from their mother

    in a captive breeding program.

            I want to touch my face
over and over again.

            To take you with me

so we can rub ourselves
with fungus, lie between cracks in rocks,

                and wait for smoke to emerge from a bottle.

To finally get our wish. To be that smoke.

I sewed my sexual fantasies onto leaves
            (the fantasies that involve my
scrambling to reinsert
                all the orbs spilling out from my chest—
        all the orbs whose collective sum
                    signifies my age);

    ripped them up,

along with the fabric softener you pulled out
        from inside your sweater (only to find a bee);

            and scattered the pieces near every
        notable meteorite on display I could find.

Now the mother in a captive breeding program
          has to use her hind legs
                    to push away the tadpoles

eating strings of her unfertilized eggs.

                    The tadpoles writhing in her
          reproductive foam need a chance
at the eggs too.

          All I could think to do was tape
                    a string of pearls
onto the mouth of a Freud action figure,

                    put it in a box labeled *neurotic*,
                              and place it on your doorstep.

          You remind me of an alternative:
                    the ant infected with a fungus that drives
                    it up to the highest point it can find

          so that when its head explodes,
                    spores are disseminated
to the widest extent.

I left a note in the box:
While looking for fresh produce boxes
                    to stow away into,

          a chicken frog stepped in my trail of
leaves and thread and brought back
                    the disease to his species.

When this trail touches you,
          you will roll over enough
                    for me to see your bare skin,

enough skin for me to squeeze
a small drop of water onto,

to acquire your nervous system,

to weave it with fibers growing around us
that ask for nothing but our promise

to stop thinking of ourselves
as human in any way.

When I call you a host,
stroke your chin for psychoactive venom,

search you out
and collect you again,

only to release you, only to worry about
and change your gender with pesticides again,

can you stop yourself from mounting
the resulting manifestation?

You write down my chemical signature so I won't forget.
It says: *You come from outside.*

I feel myself kick.

The Last Bulb of the Christmas Tree:
Yesterday and Today

"The LORD is God, and he has made his light to shine upon us. Bind the festal sacrifice with cords, up to the horns of the altar!"

(Psalm 118:27)

A child bound with cords underneath
a headstone says,

I shot a crop dusting rocket in the sky;
the unexploded rocket tip
landed in my chest.

When I'm supposed to think of her,

prop clouds hanging over the coliseum
catch fire; bells with cut wires ring;

women hide under Zeus' shield,
only to get raped by him first.

I ask the coroner if conventional weapons in space
look like a two-headed child
of the sun and moon
standing on a dragon
perched on the winged globe of chaos

like her body.

I was the first to discover that the Rocky Mountains grew
higher in an attempt to protect her;

at midnight it was inlaid with eyes,
front and back, that winced
then disappeared.

I knew when we placed her in the incinerator
     and the door flew open and decapitated

someone, the ancestors of the spiritual world
     accepted the offering.

The end of all flesh is come before me.[1]

This can be felt.

Stringed mannequins in the sky get shot with arrows
     so God can have a free supply of weapons.

          Only an expert could have tied those knots.

---

[1] "And God said unto Noah, '*The end of all flesh is come before me*; for the earth is filled with violence through them; and, behold, I will destroy them with the earth.'" - Genesis 6:13, *King James Bible "Authorized Version," Cambridge Edition*

MK-Ultra 1 (Monarch): Knitting a Bridge You Later Claim Is Just Over There

"Henry [Kissinger] placed the needle in between my knuckles and if I bled, he pulled out one of his fancy handkerchiefs to wipe it off . . . . It was better for both of us when he was able to replace the needle with touch programs."

Brice Taylor, *Thanks for the Memories*

The ball gag is gone.

Freeze the lock you stole
            and sit on the waltz foot pattern
      in front of your human effigy.

When the ice melts,
                  Vienna waltz towards Father.

            Ask him to bring you bottle caps.

If you make no eye contact,
                  he will also bring cow
      tongues *so you can determine*
when the bottle caps go bad—

            like we write on your genitals.

The boy who watches you arrange
                  cow tongues into the shape of a cyclone
      (your trials) brushes the corner of a blanket
                  against his neck.

He knows you stole his lock.

He wears black sweat suits covered in skeleton
            masking tape. He's always in the background
            of your photos, pointing up.

Because you begged the boy not to call you
            the mirrored soul of the underworld striving
                        for Aether while he cattle-prodded you,

                        you upset Father again,
and now he's gone.

In your cement room,
he won't be there to suction
            saliva as you color sequence bottle caps
        to recall your clientele's sexual preferences,

so put away the skull measurement device.

Go to the boy inside the cardboard dresser
            and offer a strip of your skin as a replacement
        hymen you must sew yourself.

Decide which half of your brain
            watches the direction of your clientele's masked

waltz because your seamstress log is no way
to keep anyone close

            until we say it is.

        Keep pointing up in your trance
        knitting a bridge you later claim
is just over there.

MK-Ultra 2 (Montauk): Return Me to Houyhnhnms

"Return me to yahoos." David Berkowitz

All of this began when I saw the bird
      use his beak
            as a phonograph needle.

          I could have accepted anything
     as everything else at that point,

but Iris told me a thing
      can only be its own thing.

But she never had to sew silk
     onto the inside seams of her shirt

to try and stop all the possibilities,

       like when she told me to yell
   in my bed so she could clean herself

with vigor. The way she looked at me
         up from her corn cob.

I'm not sure why the cops let me go.
I see them at our meetings.

       They wipe their noses below my window,
and I wipe mine.

I hate to see what's behind her. Iris.

I remember for sure, as a kid,

men kept saying hello to me at night,
each bringing his own coffee maker.

After days of trying to straighten my cats'
tails, I was thankful to try.

I hope everyone has a Happy Thanksgiving;
that's the main point of who I am now.

She promises I will return to the streets.
I add: *In the arms from behind.*

If I try to make my shoulder blades
touch, I feel them the least.

I will return, looking back as if to say:
There have to be other arms.

I've been sewn upon
to make all these arms.

Arms, I have to return to what I do,
though I better not.

MK-Ultra 3 (Operation Midnight Climax): Tinker Bell Also Puts Up with It in Her Own Way

"And he put forth the form of a hand and took me by a lock of my head; and the spirit lifted me up between the earth and the heaven and brought me in the visions."

(Ezekiel 8:3)

For only a quarter,
　　　Thaddeus shows me the neurolinguistic
　　　　　programming of *On the other hand,*

　　　　　an insectezoid wrapped in the American
flag of the palm like I thought.

　　　Ever since Thaddeus got a sty
after misspelling the word *sty* at a spelling bee,

I knew he wasn't like anyone else.

　　　　　On the missing piece of Pangaea
between North America and Western Europe,

　　　I place blue stones all around and anesthetize
him in a U-shaped trough.

Within a few hours
　　　　　he returns to his regular shape,
a 6-pointed merkabah double-tetrahedron

like the badges
　　　The Beatles wore at Shea Stadium
　　　　　to travel inter-dimensionally.

My DNA is losing its filler
                              but the sex:

        He sews the bag's last stitch
                    through my lips and hides me under a plank
during the duelers' vows.

                              At the base of my neck,
                         he burns an offering
                  where my second mouth snaps in hunger.

He looks at it and says:
                    My lover, he takes care of me.

        It tells him: *My experiences with oak tree*
nymphs have not just been sexual.

Things keep getting better and better,
        especially after I find myself
restrained by electromagnetic currents.

        I know the 1984 Chrysler LeBaron says:
                    The door is ajar
and *Fasten your safety belts,*

but it also says: *The best*
            photograph I have of you
                    was taken before you knew
            what cameras are.

Human fingers, Christianizing,

                    pull me into starships
            hovering in Saturn's debris
field (as documented by the Cassini space probe).

Tinker Bell also puts up with it
in her own way.

Puteum Abyssi: *Till I Get to the Bottom and I See You Again*

"You may think of Sexy Sadie/Let her in through your front door/And your life won't be so easy anymore."

"Simply Shady" George Harrison

Darryl, most of the names the dying
        man screamed actually exist
in Norse mythology.

        I should know;
     as a boy at the hospital,
I was starving so much
     I could have been hung up on a hook.

Rudi decorated the walls
     with baby bones
     he found under an ancient whorehouse
way before he ever met me,

     so I felt fated
to become his resident caretaker.

Ask the police to check the bones'
     arrangement to see if the three men
knocking on the door
     begging to use the phone

were actually searching all over
     for a hole the Hopis said
     contains a river flowing northward.

     I had to picture the plainclothes man
on a horse-drawn lawn mower
in order to comfort myself,

and now my days
last twice as long as yours.

Also tell my mom
something killed the normal
flora on my hands

when I held the three-eyed baby
the men gave to me at gunpoint.

She told me: *The double spiritual power
of twin murder is the natural surface
and form of their silhouettes.*

It wasn't long before the suited
men stuffed my mouth full of pills
and ordered me not to quit,
or *wring out* as the Navy Seals call it.

One of them said, repeat after me:
*That's how I killed those people—
through a tent.*

I bet their mommies never made them
silver dollar pancakes.

Out the window, I saw a woman running
across Russia until her kneecaps
were on the opposite side.

She screamed: *Stop stabbing;
I'm already dead.*

I'll fail the polygraph, though,
because one picture can be a tea cup,
mug, or coffee cup.

I plan to walk around the estate until daybreak,
        suturing them all myself,
                but I don't need the tendons.

You know me, Darryl,
I used to do a little macramé in my day.

The Hopis said the men are the type
                        who will kill a goldeneye
        and call it a trout

for no other reason than just to fool
the L.A. boys.

                I touch her bone
        because no one else ever does.

Marilyn Monroe's First Miscarriage Lives on Colfax Avenue

"Forever Hollywood's sweetheart, Marilyn poses glamorously by a velvet rope inside this splendid Marilyn Monroe Musical Water Globe. The sphere sits on a film-strip base that plays the memorable 'Candle in the Wind' song!"

Marilyn Monroe Velvet Rope Musical Water Globe description

Hustleman Joe tussles a college boy and asks:
How do you turn a sphere inside out?

Joe answers: *Never tear it. Never crease it.*
Tell it it's special. Get it to pass through itself.

All the men were told never to bruise
Mama, but she did give birth to a Black baby
and got filled with sawdust
from a psychoanalyst who took me away.

Like Thoth, he harnesses the power to move
both light and dark.

Outside of Hollywood,
men let themselves go.
To stop them from finding the symbols
cut into my skin—

the same maps burned into desert rock
to be seen from space
after Armageddon—

I hold a red light up to my body.

My way of not giving them permission
to return. One Hong Kong businessman
said I was created from a cord
being dragged through the mud.

No, not a cord, I tell him:
... *FBI-grade surveillance wires* . . . .

Joe didn't believe my story
            until I went to Monroe Liquors,
        counted to reach the door's
                    sixth bar from the left, pulled it back,

and accepted the cache
of gang-designated weapons
            the governor gave me to distribute.

            Joe grabbed his best girl Pearl,
        put a pill in her mouth, and said,
            It's because of Marilyn's sixth toe, Baby.

He could never guess
that once when Mama was placed
            in the outstretched arms of a statue,

                an initiate slaughtered a bull—
        but not Mama as the High Priest ordered.

In her diaries she wrote it was the closest
she ever felt to being loved.

The man told me
        he was actually just hypnotized
                    to think the animal was her.

I know Mama loved me

    because when I was stolen,
                she called me a doll
        whose hair was taken from the last Ice Age
woman who has no DNA match in modernity.

Her way of pleading, *Let the dead be.*

Xennials

"We 'Xennials,' born somewhere in between *Halloween* and *A Nightmare on Elm Street*, make up an unclaimed, misfit micro-generation, the poor suckers in the middle—first given a sweet taste of the good life, and then kicked in the face."

Jed Oelbaum

My career has made a turn.

In the makeshift conference room,
     I do conceptual work for a wider audience,
a work requiring a military
       center of gravity behind closed doors,

       a parasitism, a chip clip sealing my side.

The book publisher says: *Write my name as Jein*[2]
for Jesus and incubus
       or Jezebeth and incisors.

He projects film clips of American, Canadian,
     British, and Australian droughts
through auto-presencing,

       the first language,

which is how I communicate every Thursday
     when I get my allergy shots.

He does well with plastics too.

     The energies from our partnership
are either zoned as a business

---

[2] German for "yes and no."

or killed to prevent
a worldwide information leak,

possibilities which are actualized through my ingestion
                of *Budae jjigae* (army stew) and *lye.*

Every day I just bite a belt
                and hope for the best.

                Proof of how I have been rewarded
can be found in the vault
                under the Parliament House of Finland
where my cranial measurements are now stored.[3]

All because I was chosen.

These days network public relations departments
put my hands out the window at night
                so I can pick up lunar energies,

but I still eat nothing but hotdogs and Spam
                taken from U.S. Army facilities,

                        and the workers still leave
            the unlabeled bags of lye
next to the unlabeled bags of sugar.

I'm trying to get my name out there more
                        no matter what.

As a child, I was called down
            to the principal's office to have a drink,

                and nothing was the same again.

---

[3] PhD graduates in Finland have their head (hat) measurements
stored in a vault under the House of Parliament.

The woman who conducted the experiments,
        I loved her in that way boys
must never love their own mothers
                                but do.

        Is it ejaculation or self-castration
                        that creates worlds?
I leaned over to see my progress report
                and both items were checked off.

        There, barbs attached themselves to my ethereal
matter like you wouldn't believe,

        and it's because one day I found Debbie
                        in the aquarium.

        A white paper bag. With the arms
cut off. She drowned herself
        (insofar as a member of that family can die)
                just as a way to socialize with me.

        Has she fused to him yet? someone asked
through the 2'x 2' sliding wall compartment
                before I woke up in another country.

Every Xennial I meet has a similar sob story.

Smoking Test Cigarettes (Labeled *X*, *Queen of Diamonds*, or *Daisy*) for Some Easy Cash

"Don't you draw the Queen of Diamonds, boy, she'll beat you if she's able."
"Desperado" The Eagles

When the peanuts slip out of the hole
in my gown, I'm bound to them all
      by string. They spell messages like:

              If my missing has a tongue . . . .

I open my mouth, feel it, and extract it,
        a wooden skewer stuck through the back
    of my throat.

Because it leaves my hand as a blue feather
            and then mist, I say:
I had been filled with another spirit,
not my own.

This shows I am a young man
    trying to learn how to become an artist
        like in Ancient Greece,

but for now I smoke test cigarettes (labeled *X*,
    Queen of Diamonds, or *Daisy*)
for some easy cash.

My older lover Michael stays with me at the hospital
     and wears a shirt that says "America's Heartland"
     with a Valentine's Day heart outlining
a bombed building. He's a frontman,

      and we call where we live "the jar city."

He tells me of the little people of the world,
the ones fixing up old Detroit muscle cars
    who have brain ventricles that look like butterflies

or his wife whom he models after a 1690
                    hermaphrodite wearing rope tights,
    undoing her robe.

Last month when money was tight,
I smoked a Queen of Diamonds
                    and walked right out
of the Central Park Lagoon.

When I delivered powder-filled baggies
        to musicians, I was so nervous around them
I kept saying *Atticus*
                    when I meant *Gregory Peck.*

Not only that, I stayed the night at the YMCA,
            and the faucet that releases a pulverized
                        body of a man,

like what's in kitchens,
                    was above the night stand.

Michael stood naked next to the bed,
        poured himself a glass, and said:

You are a victim of a group of doctors.[4]

All night I could only walk along the edges
                    of the room,
my back against the wall.

---

[4] Jansen, Bart. "Bomb implants? Not too likely." *USA Today* 14 June 2012. Web. 18 July 2014. "Marigot, 41, a French citizen born in Cameroon, gave a crewmember a note that said she was the 'victim of a group of doctors' and that she had 'an object in her body that is out of (her) control,' according to U.S. Attorney Thomas Delahanty."

When I could, I contacted a Tianjin
        funeral agent who charged me ¥3000
                to have a woman wail for ten minutes
        at the glass.

Michael keeps me financially dependent on him,
        but I still love him.

Some days our relationship is like this:
        Michael stretches an authentic African Wild Dog
                hide over a body form.

        There's me, Michael, and the fine being
        who exists as a better version of me
between us, but it works.

Did I just say that or is it just me?

The Best Way to Go Is by M&DC: Takedowns Are All Metal

"Maxwell's silver hammer made sure John was dead."

Sir Paul, *Let it Be* Sessions

It's true I took a special interest in my own face in the mirror. I wonder how Sue sees it with all her multiple data calculations to consider. I can only gather clues from the way she blushes, types with perfect posture, and has a blue ribbon tied around her blonde ponytail.

When God told me to plead guilty, Sue received a memo, and on the giant screen, someone zoomed in on my body until the only visible thing was an ingrown hair. At this vital time with God in my ear and Satan trying to derail me from another cell, my imperfection was there for Sue to see—a test of sorts. I know her whole story. Her father was a student in her mother's Spanish class. Their grief over John's death threw them into each other's arms, and then there was Sue.

The night of the shooting itself, Maxwell was behind a staircase a few blocks away pointing a hammer at me saying: *The Catcher in the Rye says John Lennon must die.* He had his gun on a tripod aimed at the Dakota in case I messed up, which I did. The doorman was in and out of the control center in my mind, fiddling with an abacus, making calls, and slamming down the phone, but he was mainly sketching with oil pencils. He drew a picture of apron-wearing assassins kicking Edgar Allan Poe to death. *Pull your apron tight,* he chanted at me.

In person, the doorman asked me which assassination was my favorite, and I said, *All of them!* I failed the mission because I ran up to John to tell him the same person who used to talk to him in the mirror, the one who said *Soon John, soon* with regards to his fame, was also talking to me. That's what I thought this thing was going to be about because the man in the mirror said so, but then the doorman took his shot—Yoko way ahead. The way everyone in the control center cheered for me and threw up their clipboards made me feel responsible.

When Sue was born, I watched it all on the screen, and I swear Yoko was there too, forty paces ahead of Sue's crowning. Sir Paul said *Takedowns are all metal* when he handed her to Dr. D. Ewen Cameron, president of the Canadian Psychological Association (the boss here).

When I sign a copy of *The Catcher in the Rye,* please be Sue when I get a partial erection because something touches the inside of my urethra.

Magnetic Fields on the Road to Damascus, a May to December Marriage

"John wrote *Skywriting* at a time when the world was wondering whatever happened to him. Why wasn't he writing songs anymore? Well, this was what he was busy doing."

Yoko Ono

When a Gauloises Bleues burns
　　　　　down in my hand, I peel off
　　another Japanese robe,

　　　　　the extra personalities I splay on beds
with bloody nails bought from flea markets,
　　　　nine inches long.

The figures' polymorphic curves
　　　　catch the overhead light,

the tracers of the Goddess Columbia stringing
　　　　　telegraph wires across the ceiling.

　　　　Go west to the Dakotas, she intones
　　and rattles her tail.

I immediately build my own Aeolian harp
　　　　so I can reason with her.

　　　　　I'm sure you're familiar with high-tensile
electrical fences that keep sheep in?

I can even feel some of my umbilical cords
　　　　drying up and falling off
when the TV evangelist's Bible
　　　　emits curtains to strangulate me.

This prompts Goddess Nuwa to fix a rip
in the sky in the white room
                    by blocking it with her body.

Her snake-like lower-half
            conducts my piano playing,
        while something else shaves my leg

for surgery—a decorative gargoyle.

                    One of my personalities greets it,
                        my right temporal lobe

        that accepts any kind of beam
from space, the concept of myself

            the brain interprets as Elvis.

I became aware of him as myself
when the gold rings on my fingers
                    turned my hands black.

Prairie dogs, pheasants, upright
        walking reptiles as big as me
                        trailing my moves.

The idea for manifest destiny didn't just happen.

A light reaches me that excites my cells;
            the plastic threads melt into coils

                into Brazilian coffee
I drink twenty to thirty times a day.

Who are you, Lord? I ask Yoko.
                Did I mention that cats always seem extra
                            sexually attracted to me?

I wake up naked next to my love
who's wearing a business suit.

I scrambled your DNA,
but it was for the best,
she says with a mouth
full of Christmas tree bulbs.

She asks me to plug in the tree, and I do
as I watch her mouth for my lighted
signal to fall, convulse,

and go blind with my love
(that she and the help attest)
is for her and only her.

A Maple Gets Red

Wearing his long brown hair in Gibraltar, maybe he is not one of my relatives, but when I think of him, a tall, thin, castrated old man appears before my eyes. This is what she sees in him, that he will chase the great mass fervor. Perhaps I can pound his back to offer him a massage.

Does he use her heat to warm and relief his ache? I wasn't invited to the wedding, but someone in the world has special reasons for existing who will influence you in an insidious way. They put all their body on you until the surface of the egg hardens, the bottom side turns into coke.

As saying gone, she was in every footprint of my growing up, not him. She was suddenly a figure that mapped abandoned hospitals into my eyes. It's true because I haven't been taken in by lots of bodies' hearts.

How do I feel living in the dark world? I bear her laughing. She makes my life a white paper, no color, no contains. She puts me on a ghost trolley and works for people who have power to elect whatsoever to feed me. Worst of all, I'm always hanging over heads for too long, and I know it's because of her.

Since the wedding I tell myself everyone who makes up a home with you is your wife. I will try my best to get in touch with them, form even ships with them, and ultimately live and work for them. It's not unknown to me they are pathetic and do not have a high life level. They cheat for money or robot for money, but I can learn too.

A maple gets red, and it's not too late for me to wait ten years before I act out my plan of revenge. He looks at his ring thinking he will sit in a constant seat. Their life is out of guarantee until zero o' clock—even any baby just born included.

AI Supercomputer as Black Magic Megaritual Amplifier: Sir Paul McCartney's God Given Right

"They had as king over them the angel of the Abyss, whose name in Hebrew is Abaddon and in Greek is Apollyon (that is, Destroyer)."

(Revelation 9:11)

Times New Roman of the AI supercomputer, Mesmerism,
         distressed landscape of the electrode
spike in the architect's skull,

how he designed the World Trade Center
              with a separate partition for the dynamite.

The monarch trumpet begins with the first three measures
                    of sacred programming:

(a body lying in a gold-lined box filled with briefcases,
spoiled wine, Aaron's rod);

         the arrangement of the copper and the sun's heat;

the ash of the cooked narcotic body
taken back to the temple.

The scene can be found in the architect's geometrical
                 interpretations of narcoleptic male teen
         prostitutes waking up in the Pantheon
                 of channeled gods.

A trumpet drones.

Paul McCartney watches planes
         hit towers from his grounded plane

as kids run after the smoke in an increased tempo
         of shifting light sequences

of yes/no succubae.

Paper airplanes burn in their higher throats
       three times before the attack
                 suggesting AI precognition.

When color combines with the rhythm
       of another falling body—
(prisoners in Area 51 with skewers for spines
          toppling over in a game of human Jenga),

     Queen Elizabeth spasms and heils the sun with an ankh
          cast in the reptile ovulation rhythm
at Ground Zero.

She, a flaming tarantella dancer, conjures Baphomet
       through climbing pulleys
          of dark energy transference

    until the Pope forgives the Beatles.

Fragments of 26 separate tones
        assigned to each letter of the alphabet

         run fast sentences along the pentagram,
     gradually awakening us to a new death,

a natural consequence of any sorcery process.

Mexican youths jump on Paul McCartney's tour bus
in the murderous love rhythms
       of a mathematically impossible free-fall,

revenge. To makes sense of tragedy,
one must read the depopulation score
     as a means of premature eulogy.

Good characters can only die if it advances the plot.
         Once more in a faster tempo.

Notes

"The White House Tapes" sections I, II, and V, respectively, were modeled after transcriptions of the following dialects: North America, Mexico, Sinaloa One; Europe, Russia Two; and Africa, Egypt Three from the IDEA: *International Dialects of English Archive*, http://web.ku.edu/idea/index/htm.

"Orbs Whose Collective Sum Signifies My Age": "An easier way for a highly advanced species to disseminate itself, McKenna suspected, would be through spores, the hardest organic substance, deposited on asteroids and sent spinning through the galaxy until they crash-landed on some suitable planet. To support this wild theory, he noted the peculiar shape of the psilocybin molecule. 'It is the only 4-substituted indole known to exist on earth . . . . Psilocybin has a unique chemical signature that says, I am artificial; I come from outside.'"

---Pinchbeck, Daniel. *Breaking Open the Head: A Psychedelic Journey into the Heart of Contemporary Shamanism*. New York: Broadway Books, 2003. 234.

Acknowledgments

Green Mountains Review: "I Took to Walking Down the Middle of Highways to Avoid Getting Shot"

The Wisconsin Review: "The Best Way to Go Is by M&DC: Takedowns Are All Metal"

Enizagam: "The Game," "God Wants You to Go to Jail," "A Spider-Man Must Be Born of This Earth," "Xennials"

Skidrow Penthouse: "We Must Kill All Rats Before We Can Kill Your Rats," "Smoking Test Cigarettes (Labeled *X*, *Queen of Diamonds*, or *Daisy*) for Some Easy Cash"

Zymbol: "Mayfly Satellites"

Southeast Review: "LAPD, Blue Child, and Low Daily Rates: No One Was Killed in the Square"

Fjords Review: "Marilyn Monroe's First Miscarriage Lives on Colfax Avenue," "Tie the Gamelan I'm Sending You Piece by Piece Up to the Heavens," "The Last Bulb of the Christmas Tree: *Yesterday and Today*"

Ryga: "AI Supercomputer as Black Magic Megaritual Amplifier: Sir Paul McCartney's God Given Right," "Magnetic Fields on the Road to Damascus, a May to December Marriage," "The CD Mr. X Gave to Me That Proves Everything I'm Saying Was Confiscated by the Police upon My Arrest and Sent Directly to the Ethics Department"

ICON: "*The Sect Which Pulls the Sinews*: I've Seen You Handle Cocoons"

Phoebe: "Villagers Chop Them in Half, Thinking They Are Snakes"

Wag's Revue: "Pretending to Go and Come from Heaven by Fire," "MK-Ultra 3 (Operation Midnight Climax): Tinker Bell Also Puts Up with It in Her Own Way," "All Your Best Key Chains"

The Chariton Review: "A Maple Gets Red," "Sometime Under Prague"

Oxford Poetry: "Puteum Abyssi: *Till I Get to the Bottom and I See You Again*"

The Lifted Brow and *The Lifted Brow eBook*: "The White House Tapes"

Polarity: "MK-Ultra 1 (Monarch): Knitting a Bridge You Later Claim Is Just Over There"

The Spoon River Review: "Orbs Whose Collective Sum Signifies My Age"

Arsenic Lobster: "Thorns to Rescue Their Bodies," "MK-Ultra 2 (Montauk): Return Me to Houyhnhnms"

605 Magazine: "Would Once They Aren't in the Coffer"

Read Herring: "Watching Our Other Selves from Afar and Influencing Their Course of Action by Touching Each Other for the First Time Here"

Tea Party Magazine: "Jokes about Nepalese Villages Mostly Involve Goats"

Seneca Review: "We Do This to Simulate the Function of Digestion"

Bombay Gin: "Inside a Hand Basket in the Burlesque Theater"

Beeswax Magazine: "Wondering If I'm a Descendant of the Nephilim While Lying on a Merry-Go-Round at Prentis Park"

Arabesques Review and *The American Drivel Review*: "Under John Wayne's Hat"

Poetry Bay: "Done When No Longer Pink Inside"

CPSIA information can be obtained at www.ICGtesting.com
Printed in the USA
BVOW04s0406030816

457618BV00002B/6/P